STORIES FROM ANCIENT CIVILISATIONS

Egypt

Shahrukh Husain
Illustrated by Bee Willey

Evans

Introduction

Myths are probably the earliest stories ever told. People in ancient times used them to explain everything that was important in life – how the universe was created and how the stars, sun, moon and planets appeared in the sky. To them these elements were gods, who they worshipped and who they believed controlled their lives. They wanted to keep the gods happy so that they would be kind to them.

Myths are usually about important things like birth, death and the afterlife and tend to have a moral. For example, the story of Isis and Osiris tells us how the Egyptians believed we go to the Underworld after dying. The myth warns that, like the difficult journey of Isis, life holds many struggles but if we try, we can get through them. Egyptian myths are also about the gods and how they brought order and civilisation to the world. This meant that the king or Pharaoh who ruled humans had to be someone with the power to preserve order in the same way as the gods. Myths of the first earthly king, Horus, and of Queen Hatshepsut are examples of this.

In ancient times, people travelled huge distances to search for food and shelter or to invade and conquer lands which were rich and fertile. All these people brought their own gods and myths with them. When they settled somewhere new, an exchange took place. They introduced their gods to the local people and, in turn, began to worship some of theirs. So more myths were added and old stories blended with new ones. Sometimes the same gods were called different names, for example, the god of Hermopolis, called Setekh, became Seth, the god of chaos in Heliopolis.

The most important god was the god of the sun. He was present in all of the different creation myths because without the sun there is no life. He is the chief god in the myths of the ancient cities of both Hermopolis and Heliopolis – the two main sources of the Egyptian myths and stories we know today.

Egyptian myths existed as far back as 4,300 years ago when they were recorded in hieroglyphs in the pyramids of King Wenis. These myths were meant to help the king safely into the next world and are known as the Pyramid Texts. Other myths were found on scrolls. Fortunately, these scrolls were well preserved so that today we still have a first hand picture of the lives and beliefs of the ancient Egyptians.

For Jasmine Isabella Shackle – S.H

First published in paperback in 2008 by Evans Brothers Limited
2A Portman Mansions
Chiltern Street
London W1U 6NR

Printed in China by WKT Co. Ltd

British Library Cataloguing in Publication Data
Husain, Shahrukh
    Egypt. - (Stories from Ancient civilisations)
    1. Mythology, Egyptian - Juvenile literature 2. Egypt - Civilisation - To 332 B.C. - Juvenile literature
    I. Title
    398.2'0932
    ISBN 978 0 237 53604 6

CREDITS
Series editor: Louise John
Design: Robert Walster
Artworks: Bee Willey
Production: Jenny Mulvanny

VISIT OUR WEBSITE
www.evansbooks.co.uk

STORIES FROM ANCIENT CIVILISATIONS

Egypt

Contents

The Birth of the Sun God

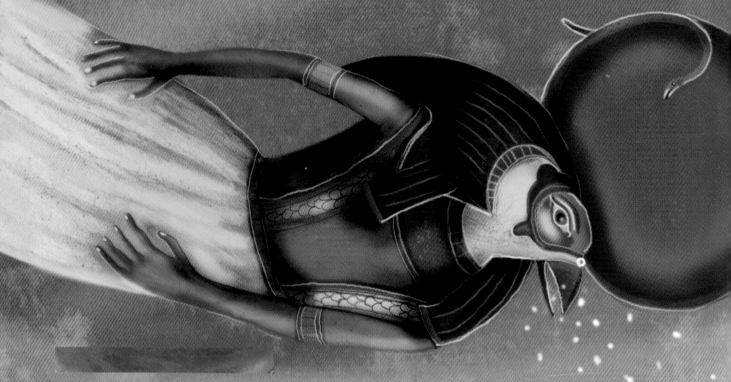

This is the story of the birth of the sun god and his offspring. Long ago ancient waters, called Neith, covered the earth. Then a mound of earth formed and grew until it stood high above the water. It gave itself a body, which glowed and shone. This was the first being to take shape and it became the sun god and creator god, Atum.

ATUM HUNCHED HIS BODY AND SNEEZED. The rush of air from his mouth became his son Shu, and from the drops came Tefnut, his daughter. Shu was air, dry and crisp. At night he shone out as the soft light of the moon and in the day he became the brightness of the sun's rays. His wife Tefnut was moisture. She was the dew at dawn and the rain of summer that nurtured the crops and she was the spray of the great river Nile that remained in the sands when the floodwaters had gone.

Shu and Tefnut were the first couple and they matched each other perfectly. Now that Atum had two children, he filled the world with gods and

goddesses, people and animals.
His work here was done and he
decided to go to the heavens, leaving
Shu and Tefnut to rule in his place.

Before going Atum reminded Shu to
respect the goddess Neith, from whom he had
come. She now lived up in the heavens in the
shape of a cow. There she held up the stars and
other planets who were also gods. Atum, the sun god,
would join them there to spread his warmth and
light. So Shu stretched out his mighty arms, one to
the east and one to the west, and he held up the
heavens containing Neith. Atum went to live in the
sky and every day he travelled the distance between
Shu's vast arms, making sure the whole world would
be warm and bright.

*The Egyptians believed that the
sun god was also the creator god.
He was called by many different
names. In Heliopolis, he was Atum.
In Hermopolis, he was Amun and
he was also often called Amun Re,
or just Re. No one knew his first
shape, though some said he had the
head of a ram. Mainly he was the
sun, bringing life to the world.*

7

How the Year Changed

Thoth, the moon god, has the head of an ibis, a bird with a crescent-shaped beak. He wears a loincloth and a long wig.

SHU AND TEFNUT WERE KING AND QUEEN OF EGYPT. They ruled wisely with their children Nut and Geb. The family of four lived happily until Atum saw how much Nut loved Geb. Suddenly he was very jealous.

'I am the one you should love most,' he scolded. 'I made you.'

But Nut still idolised Geb.

Atum grew angrier. 'I will make Geb the Earth and Nut the sky,' he bellowed, 'as far from each other as possible.'

But even from this great distance Nut and Geb adored each other. Geb, the earth, gazed up at Nut, who formed her body into a great arch and protected him as she gazed down lovingly.

Atum did not like to be ignored. He put a curse on Nut and Geb, saying, 'You cannot have children on any day of any month in the year.'

At last Nut took her eyes off Geb, 'But why, mighty Atum?' she asked, troubled.

'Because,' replied Atum, smugly, 'if you have children you will have even less time for me.'

Nut and Geb were very sad. Nut wept and her tears fell to the ground like soft rain. Thoth, the moon god, who hung in the sky, which was Nut, saw her weeping every night. He felt sorry for her and, being the cleverest god, he came up with an idea to help Nut.

'I challenge you all to a game of dice,' he told the other gods. 'If I win, you must give me what I ask for.'

The gods finally agreed and the game began.

Throw after throw of the dice, skilful Thoth won the highest score. When at last all the gods had played and lost, Thoth sat back contented.

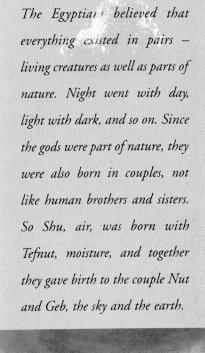

The Egyptians believed that everything existed in pairs – living creatures as well as parts of nature. Night went with day, light with dark, and so on. Since the gods were part of nature, they were also born in couples, not like human brothers and sisters. So Shu, air, was born with Tefnut, moisture, and together they gave birth to the couple Nut and Geb, the sky and the earth.

'Do you all agree I have won?' he asked.

'You are the uncontested winner,' they agreed.

'Name your wish,' Atum commanded. 'It will be granted.'

'Supreme Father,' said Thoth, 'I wish for five days to add to the year.'

'Five extra days shall be yours,' replied Atum.

'But what will you do with them, Thoth?' the gods asked. 'There are twelve months, each of thirty days, in the year already. When the moon is a crescent in the sky, we know the new month has begun. When it grows full, it is the middle of the month and as it starts to disappear, we know the end of the month is near. Where will you put your five new days?'

Thoth did not tell anyone about his secret mission. He took the five days, thanked the gods for being good sports and made his way back to Nut.

'You can stop weeping,' he said gently. 'I have a gift for you.'

'Thank you, Thoth,' Nut sighed, without interest.

'I have brought you five days, which I won from the gods in a game of dice,' he prompted.

'But what will I do with five days?' the sky goddess asked flatly.

'Don't you see?' Thoth said, grinning widely. 'These days do not belong to any month. On each of these five days, you are free to give birth.'

Nut raised up her face and began to laugh and her joy and thanks echoed through the universe. Thoth, moon god, god of wisdom, began glowing deeply, and the stars glittered and shone.

Up above, Nut's father, Shu sparkled and shimmered and rained down his light on all of Egypt.

Nut was happier than she had ever been and she gave birth to two couples.

The first pair was Isis and Osiris and the second pair was Seth and Nephthys. Later Isis and Osiris gave birth to Horus, and Seth and Nephthys bore Anubis.

Together, nine of the gods of Hermopolis came to be known as the 'Ennead', which means 'Group of Nine'. They were Neith, Atum, Shu, Tefnut, Geb, Nut, Isis, Osiris and Seth. They later became the best-known gods and goddesses of ancient Egypt.

Gods and Goddesses of Ancient Egypt

Atum (Amun Re), creator god and sun god

Hathor, cow goddess and daughter of Re

Tefnut, goddess of moisture, twin and wife of Shu

Shu, god of air, twin and husband of Tefnut

Nut, goddess of the sky, twin and wife of Geb

Geb, god of the earth, twin and husband of Nut

Isis, goddess of nature, the moon and healing, twin and wife of Osiris

Osiris, god of agriculture, the sun and the Underworld, twin and husband of Isis

Nephthys, twin and wife of Seth

Seth, god of the desert, darkness and chaos, twin and husband of Nephthys

Horus, god of the sky and earthly king of Egypt

Anubis, god of death and funerals

Isis and Osiris

This story is about the repeating cycles of nature – the four seasons. The death of Osiris explains the winter months when it is cold and there is not much growth because the sun is weak. The disappearance of Isis explains the absence of the moon for ten days each month.

WHEN GEB, THE SKY GOD, DECIDED TO LEAVE HIS KINGDOM, HIS SON OSIRIS TOOK HIS PLACE AS KING. Osiris was kind and wise. He taught the world the secret of growing crops and he brought music and dance to the world. Everyone loved him and his wife Isis, who knew magic and used it to heal people and do good. Only Osiris' brother Seth, was unhappy. He wanted to be king himself.

Seth hatched a nasty plan. He invited Osiris to a banquet and placed a large coffin, called a sarcophagus, in the centre of the room. It was covered in gold, lined with silver and studded with precious stones.

Seth chuckled, 'It is a prize for one of my guests. The person who it fits best may take it home.'

Delighted, the guests climbed in, one by one. Some were too fat, some too thin and most too short.

'Brother Osiris,' Seth smiled, slyly. 'Why don't you try your luck?'

Osiris climbed in and lowered himself into the

bottom of the sarcophagus. Instantly, Seth slammed down the lid and his men secured it with iron bands held together with heavy locks.

'Fling Osiris into the Nile,' he crowed. 'He will drown and I can be king.'

Soon Isis heard the news. 'Seth will not get away with this,' she swore. 'I will find Osiris and bring him back.'

Osiris was the sun and Isis was the moon. With one dead and the other full of grief, the earth grew dark. Because there could be no crops without light, the world became dry and nothing grew anymore. But Isis did not care. She kept on searching for Osiris until one day she arrived at a temple on the banks of the kingdom of Babylon, ruled by King Malchus and Queen Astarte. Isis walked along the riverbank. Suddenly she stopped. She could smell ambrosia, a perfume special to the gods. Her heart leapt. Osiris was nearby. She looked all around her, following the scent until she came to a ditch in the sand where the scent was strong. Isis could see a tree

Osiris is often seen as a mummy, wearing a crown and carrying a crook and a flail to show he is a king. Often he is shown as part of a pillar. His double crown contains the sun disc.
Seth is often seen with either the body of a man or a four-legged animal.

had once grown there.

'Whoever dug up that tree knows where to find Osiris,' she thought excitedly. 'But how will I find out who that is?'

She sat down on the fountain near the temple. Deep in thought, she did not hear Queen Astarte's chariot draw up.

'Who are you, sad lady?' the queen asked, stepping out of the chariot.

'I am a stranger in search of my husband,' Isis replied, 'but I do not know who can help me.'

'Come with me,' said Astarte, 'you can live in the palace and work for me while you look.'

So Isis found herself in Astarte's palace, looking after the little prince of Babylon. One day as she carried the baby into the main hall, Isis smelled ambrosia again. She looked around and her eye fell upon a wooden pillar.

The Egyptians believed that the sprouting of a seed is like the birth of a baby. Its growth from young plant to ripe crop is like a child growing up. It produces new grain as people bear children. Being harvested is like dying. With replanting, the cycle begins all over again. They believed it was the same for humans.

'That is the tree that they dug up,' she thought. The sarcophagus carrying Osiris had been washed on to the shores of Babylon and come to rest against a young tamarisk tree. As the tree grew, its trunk surrounded Osiris and stopped the sarcophagus being washed away, keeping him safe. In return, Osiris filled the tree with his perfume. The king's men, smelling the rare perfume, had cut it down and given it as a gift to the king.

Isis knew she had to cut Osiris out from the tree but King Malchus had looked after Osiris and Queen Astarte had brought her to the palace and she wanted to reward them.

'I will make their son live forever,' she decided. Isis turned herself into a bird and stirred the air until a magic fire blazed around the baby. It would burn away the threads that made people human. That way, he would become immortal and join the gods. The spell took many days to work. Every night Isis waited until the palace was asleep. Then she began her magic. At last, the spell was nearly complete. But, just as it was coming to its end, Astarte walked in and saw the fire blazing with her baby boy in the middle of it.

Astarte snatched her child from the flames in fear and panic. 'I was kind to you and you nearly killed my child,' she wept.

'Your child was perfectly safe,' Isis replied. 'I am the goddess Isis. I was trying to repay you by making your son immortal. But you have spoiled my spell.'

Just then the king entered. 'Oh mighty goddess!' he cried, recognising the magic powers of Isis and falling to his knees. 'Please forgive my wife. Tell me how I can win back your mercy.'

Isis took pity on the king. 'You have a tamarisk pillar that I would like very much,' she smiled.

Malchus ordered the pillar to be cut open as Isis commanded. Inside was the sarcophagus of Osiris. She opened the lid impatiently, wanting to speak to Osiris, but he was still and silent. Isis thought he was dead. But then Osiris spoke in a serious and distant voice.

'Re, my grandfather, is the sun and Shu, my father, holds up the skies. Now, as the kings before me, it is my turn to serve the universe,' he said.

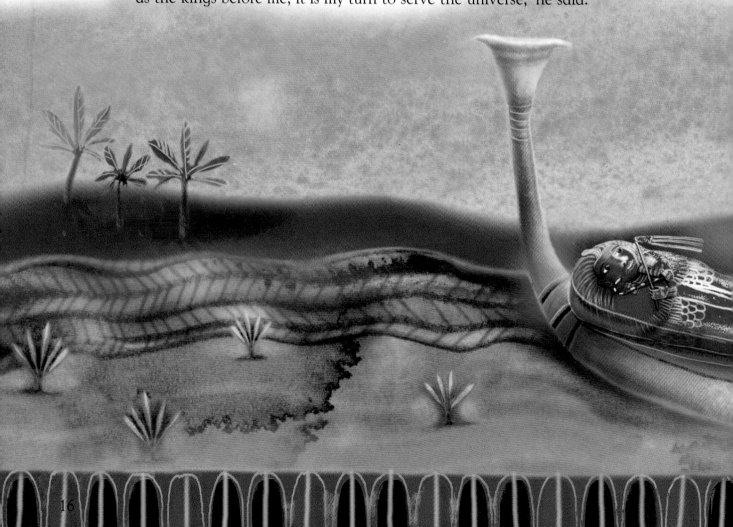

'What will you do?' Isis asked.

'I am going to live in Duat, the Underworld. I will be god of eternal life,' replied Osiris. 'It will be my job to make sure that those who have been good will live again after death. You will give birth to our son soon and he will rule Egypt in my place.'

Isis was sad that Osiris was going away but she was happy that he was not dead. She placed the sarcophagus containing his body on a boat and made her way to Egypt.

Isis knew that Osiris would rise each morning in the Underworld and give new life to all the plants that had withered and died while he was lost. The grain would grow again. The flowers would bloom. Once again the sounds of laughter would fill the air. And Isis would recognise the work of Osiris in all those things.

Egyptian myths often include opposite symbols to show the world must be in balance. In this story Osiris is good and stands for order and fertile valleys while Seth is evil and stands for chaos and the barren desert. When Seth kills Osiris, the world loses its balance. When Osiris fulfils his new function as god of eternal life, order is restored.

The First Mummy

This story is about mummification. The Egyptians believed that after people died they moved on to the Underworld to live a new life. That is why it was important to preserve people's bodies and they did this by mummifying them. The words and paintings on the walls of tombs and pyramids were also intended to help people pass into the Underworld.

Isis brought back the body of Osiris from Babylon and laid the sarcophagus by the mouth of the river in the Delta of Khemmis, the most fertile part of Egypt. She knew that if Seth discovered Osiris' body there, he would destroy it to make sure Osiris did not return to claim his throne. Isis knew it was useless trying to explain that Osiris' work in this world was finished and he had moved to the Underworld to rule Duat, so she hid the sarcophagus in the reeds and rushes by the river.

One day when Isis was out looking for food, Seth arrived in Khemmis with a hunting party. He tramped through the rushes where Osiris was hidden, looking for prey to shoot with his deadly arrows. Instead, he stumbled on the sarcophagus. He recognised it immediately.

'I will get rid of him forever,' he crowed. Seth and his men cut Osiris up into fourteen parts and scattered them throughout Egypt.

Isis was full of grief when she found Osiris gone. Nephthys, Seth's wife, told Isis what had happened and promised that she would help her.

Duat was the Underworld, which Osiris ruled after he left the human world. Plants and creatures go to Duat after dying and are reborn later. Amun, the sun god, journeys through Duat every night leaving the world dark. He later returns to bring day to the world.

They travelled all over Egypt looking for the pieces of Osiris' body. When they finally found them all and put them together, they asked Anubis, the son of Nephthys, for his help. Anubis wrapped the mended body in strips of linen to hold Osiris together to enter the Underworld whole. Soon afterwards, Anubis became known as the protector of the dead and Osiris was the first-known mummy.

Myths of the Eye

The Sacred Eye is an ancient Egyptian symbol of cosmic order and protection and there are many myths written on the subject. This story about the roaming eye of Atum is about how Hathor, a goddess of love and daughter of Atum, came to be part of the later myths of Heliopolis.

For the Egyptians, the left eye was the lunar eye, or the moon eye, and the right one was the solar eye, or the sun eye. Both were shown with two lines below them, representing the tears of Atum, which turned into people. Often, the eyes were decorated with cobras, other snakes or wings. The moon eye was set in a boat with the moon disc, as well as three sun gods, Re, Osiris and Horus, above it.

The Roaming Eye of Atum

ATUM, THE FATHER OF THE GODS, WAS SAD. He had spent many lonely years in the waters of chaos before turning himself into a god and creating his children, Shu and Tefnut. Now they had wandered away and he was alone again.

'I will create a daughter from my eye,' he decided. 'I will call her Hathor. She will find them for me.'

Hathor looked everywhere for Atum's children. Shu was air and Tefnut was moisture and both were hard to see. So she watched the breezes as they blew and the morning dew fall upon the leaves, until at last she found them and brought them back to their father.

'Oh my children, my children,' Atum rejoiced. 'I'm so glad you have come back to me.' He held them close. Tears of happiness welled up in his eyes and they fell to the earth and became the first people.

Then Atum turned to Hathor, 'As a reward,' he said, smiling his thanks, 'I will turn you into an eye and place you on my forehead for all to see and admire.'

Atum kept his promise and the eye is found all over Egypt in ancient paintings and good luck charms made from silver, copper and brass. Pictures of the eye have been framed and hung in homes for good luck ever since then.

Hathor was the cow goddess and represented joy, beauty, love and marriage. Most other goddesses that were in the form of a cow were connected with Hathor and this meant that they were also considered to be kind and happy goddesses.

The Vengeful Eye of Amun Re

In Egypt there was a time when people were wiped out by drought because the Nile didn't flood. People believed that Sekhmet's attack in the story of the Vengeful Eye explains this destruction of the people of Egypt. Pharaoh Tutankhamun himself believed that the gods had abandoned Egypt and brought it to ruin, and he tried hard to win back their favour.

AMUN RE HAD GROWN OLD. He decided to leave the city of Thebes in Hermopolis and become the sun. People began to mock him. Amun Re grew angry.

'How dare they make fun of me? What if I am old?' he ranted.

The gods spoke calming words, 'You are not like ordinary people,' they comforted him. 'Their skins wither and wrinkle but yours glows pure gold. Human bones bend and weaken with age while yours are solid silver. Your beard is the precious and sacred gemstone, lapis lazuli, but age greys the beards of men and makes them drop away. These people speak nonsense.'

'Still,' Re insisted. 'They must learn to respect their creator.'

So Amun Re summoned Hathor. 'Find the people who make fun of me,' he commanded, 'and punish them. And because you are a gentle goddess, I will give you a fierce side. When you find the people who mock me, you will become Sekhmet, the lioness.'

Hathor bowed low and set off on her journey. She found the people who made fun of her father. In a flash she became Sekhmet the lioness and tore apart the offenders. Then, with blood still on her fangs, she attacked again. Amun Re summoned her back.

'I will rest a while,' she said proudly, 'then I will go back and destroy more people. I like the taste of blood.'

Sekhmet's words shocked Amun. 'I wanted the people punished,' he thought, 'not destroyed altogether.'

Amun had to stop Sekhmet. He came up with a plan.

'Bring the earth from the Red Land of Upper Egypt,' he commanded his gods, 'and mix it with seven thousand jugs of barley wine. Pour them into the fields where Sekhmet will see the wine.'

Sekhmet awoke, stretched and made her way down to earth. Below, she saw fields overflowing with red liquid.

'Blood!' she roared. Immediately she flew down and began to drink greedily. Very soon the wine made her drowsy, and she fell into a deep, deep sleep. When she awoke, the Sekhmet part of Hathor was calm and she returned to heaven, once again her happy, helpful self.

The story of Sekhmet was found in Pharaoh Tutankhamun's tomb when it was discovered in 1922 after remaining untouched for 3,300 years. Tutankhamun was buried with an array of precious gold and jewelled objects, as well as all the things he would have needed for the afterlife, such as clothes, furniture and even chariots.

The Shining Eye of Horus

Horus was the sky god and earthly King of Egypt. He was often shown as a falcon soaring high in the sky. He was believed to appear in the skies every July in the form of the constellation Orion, causing the Nile to flood so that the crops would have water and grow. The story of the Shining Eye of Horus tells us the reason why the moon (which was said to be one of Horus' eyes) disappears for around ten days of every month.

HORUS WAS CALLED THE 'FAR-ABOVE ONE' BECAUSE HE WAS THE SKY FALCON. One of his eyes was the sun and the other was the moon. Horus was the son of Isis and Osiris, Lord of the Underworld, and he was set to be king of Egypt. So when he was old enough, he went to his Uncle Seth to claim his throne.

'Never,' said Seth, 'you are just a boy. I will not give you my throne.'

Horus went to the rest of the gods to seek help. His great-grandfather Amun Re, who was still head of the Council of Gods, was on Seth's side. All the other gods believed that Horus should be king.

'Instead of sitting around arguing, let's fight it out,' Seth challenged. So they fought but neither side won or lost. The struggle raged on. Then, one day, when Horus lay asleep in a field, Seth crept up on him. He gouged the moon eye out of Horus' head and flung it away with all his might.

Immediately the night sky was plunged into darkness.

The gods and goddesses searched hard for the eye but they could not find it anywhere. In the end, they all gave up except Thoth, the moon god, who was determined to return it to Horus. Sadly, when he did finally find the eye, it was broken. Slowly, patiently, he began to piece it together. Then he said a spell to make all the cracks disappear.

'I have brought back your eye,' he told Horus. 'Now you can see again and light will return to the night sky.'

Horus was very happy to have his eye back. And from that day on, the healed moon eye became known as 'Wedjat'.

It is meant to heal people and protect them from harm.

The Birth of Queen Hatshepsut

This is the story of the birth of Pharaoh Hatshepsut, the first female Pharaoh of Egypt. The story is told in pictures on the walls of Hatshepsut's temple to Amun Re at Deir al-Bahri. Hatshepsut was born in 1504 BCE and died in 1482 BCE. She wore the false stone beard of wisdom used by all Pharaohs. Her story shows how myths and history blended together over the course of time.

Isis is the best known goddess of Egypt. On her crown is the Egyptian hieroglyph for 'throne'. She sometimes also wears a horned crown carrying the moon disc.

AWAY IN THE KINGDOM OF THE GODS AMUN RE WAS DEEP IN THOUGHT. The others sat around him, wondering what was on his mind. At last, Amun spoke.

'Until now all the rulers of Egypt have been men. I think it is time for a change.'

'What kind of a change, Divine Father?' asked Thoth, god of wisdom.

'Isis is powerful and wise,' Amun began, 'in fact, she is the goddess of the throne of Egypt. I see now that there is no reason why a human woman should not become Pharaoh.'

The gods gaped at each other in wonder. Was this wise? There had never been a female Pharaoh before. Plenty of queens, but not a single Pharaoh. Since ancient times, the queen was traditionally the person to inherit the throne but it was her husband who always became Pharaoh. It was believed that the spirit of Amun, which was said to be present in all kings, helped them to rule well.

Isis' laughter broke the shocked silence. 'Look at your long faces,' she said. 'What is wrong with having a female Pharaoh? I am willing to guide her myself.'

Isis was a favourite of the gods. She played her sistrum and smiled and joked with them until, finally, they all agreed.

'But,' insisted Thoth to Amun, 'she must have a part of Amun in her just like the male Pharaohs. You must place a female baby in the belly of the wife of the present Pharaoh, Thuthmosis the First, while she sleeps. You will create this baby, who shall be known as your daughter, so that her great qualities will shine out for all to see. In time, she will naturally find her place as Pharaoh.'

The very next day, Amun arrived at the palace and made his way to the chamber of Ahmosis, the wife of the Pharaoh. Standing beside her, he created a tiny bud, which would one day flower into a great woman.

Amun was the chief god of Hermopolis. He wears a tall crown with feathers. In Thebes, he joined with Khnum, who had a ram's head. In Heliopolis he merged with Re and became Amun Re, who had the shape of a human with the head of a hawk. He is also shown as the sun.

The Egyptians believed that there was a part of Amun Re in all Pharaohs and that was why Pharaohs were respected as gods. As a woman, Hatshepsut had to prove she deserved the same respect. That is probably why she told this story.

Immediately the room was filled with an exquisite scent. It was a smell more wonderful than flowers or herbs or any scent known to man. It was the perfume of the gods themselves. And, as he placed the bud in Ahmosis, she too, became filled with this glorious scent.

As the baby grew, the whole palace was filled with the wonderful perfume of the gods. When at last she was born, the Pharaoh, her earthly father, named her Hatshepsut, which means, 'part of the best', because he knew she was a gift from the gods.

Much later, as Amun had foretold, Hatshepsut became the first female Pharaoh.

Glossary

ambrosia – a special substance belonging to the gods. It produced a heavenly fragrance.

chaos – when order breaks down. For example, when the rains don't come, there is no harvest and everything becomes barren. People, animals and plants die of hunger and thirst.

constellation – any of 88 groups of stars, as seen from Earth. Many of these groups were named after animals, mythological persons or objects.

council of gods – a gathering of the senior gods and goddesses.

creator god – the god who created the world, nature and living things.

destruction – the act of destroying, ruining or causing damage to a person, place or thing.

drought – a long period where there is no rainfall, causing a shortage of water.

Duat – the world of the dead where people go after they have died in the human world, often known as the Underworld.

Ennead – a group of nine gods. In Egyptian mythology these were the nine most powerful gods of Heliopolis.

eternal life – life without end. Some cultures believe this means that people's lives are not finished when they die. Instead, they enter another world. Often, after being in the other world for a time, they may be reborn and return to the human world.

fertile – used here to describe land or soil that contains lots of goodness and plants and crops grow very well.

Heliopolis – an ancient Egyptian city around which many myths were written. Dates to around 3000 BCE and means 'City of the Sun'.

Hermopolis – an ancient Egyptian city in Middle Egypt, meaning 'Island of Flames'. It was called 'Khemnu' by the ancient Egyptians and is called 'Al-Ashmunein' today.

hieroglyph – a picture symbol representing a word or words, as used in ancient Egypt.

immortal – having everlasting life. An immortal person will never die.

lapis lazuli – a blue gem stone with silver or gold veins. In the ancient world it was treasured as a sacred stone. Gods and goddesses used it in their rituals.

lunar cycle/calendar – the organising of the months according to the movements of the moon.

mummy – a body that is prepared for burial by having its organs removed and filled with preservatives to keep it fresh for a long time. The body was wrapped firmly together with white bandages.

order – the balanced, organised way in which the universe works. For example, day always follows night, summer always follows spring, the river always floods its banks in the rainy season and the crops always produce a harvest.

solar cycle/calendar – the organising of the months and years according to the movements of the sun.

sarcophagus – a large, and usually highly decorated, coffin in which dead people (mummies) were placed for burial.

tamarisk – an ornamental tree found in Mediterranean regions.

Underworld – the world of the dead where people go after they have died in the human world, sometimes known as 'Duat'.

vengeful – describes a person who wants to take revenge against another person.

Wedjat – the mythical Egyptian 'moon eye' that is believed to protect people and keep them from harm.

Index